No Breasts No Requests

Notes from DJ Booths Around the Globe

Mick DiMaria

with John Lopez

No Breasts No Requests

Copyright © 2014 by Mick DiMaria.

Designed by John Lopez   scoutidearanch.com

Every effort has been made to contact the owners of the
images in this book but one or two may have been unreachable.
We would be grateful if they care to contact us.

ISBN: 0692229000
ISBN-13: 978-0692229002

First Edition

"Being a DJ is likely one of the best possible vocations a human can achieve. You're paid to make people dance, right? But these people are usually drunk and awful. Here are their dispatches from the dance floor."

GIZMODO

Our needs are few, our pleasures are many.

The lot of the DJ, let's face it, is neither arduous nor taxing, especially when compared to that of a Kentucky miner or Bogota sewage worker. We get to play our favourite records (or MP3s or laptop jiggery-pokery, let's not get too technical about it all), we get to hang out with our buddies, we get drinks tickets and we get offered illegal consumables. Not only that, but we are often viewed, usually inexplicably, as more attractive to the ladies (and gentlemen) in the audience than the average Joe/Josephine in the street. Life is good, right? Hell, yeah.

There is another side to it all, though; a darker, more insidious element that balances out the admittedly many aforementioned advantages. Firstly, there's the DJ booth as coat check, which your friends (in particular) regard as a divine right, so that you are frequently attempting to spin tunes while balancing on top of what looks like a dry cleaners or a rummage sale.

You are also a prime target for the most drunk person in the club, who likes nothing more than wandering over to tell you a few jokes and, if they get half a chance, explain to you in forensic detail why they were kicked out of high school, a situation that usually ends with them demanding the microphone so, "I can MC along with you."

But my favourite is the DJ note. The DJ note is occasionally the work of men, but it's really women who are the nightclub's keenest authors. They are occasionally witty, very occasionally acerbic but even when they are frequently dumb and/or rude, they are never less than entertaining.

I can't remember when I first encountered No Breasts No Requests, but landing on its homepage gave me the overwhelming feeling of déjà vu. I felt like I'd seen these notes before. And, in some ways, I had. Like the guy who handed me a bus ticket in Room 1 at Fabric with the simple and plain weird: "Got any Lords Of The New Church?" The script might change, but the sentiment never does, though I'm somewhat sad to confess I've never received, "Can fuck you better" (not even from my wife) and entirely relieved that I've never had, "You are horrible —Everybody" plonked in my sweaty palm.

Now, thanks to No Breasts No Requests, you can take a shortcut and enter the glamorous life of a DJ. It's all here. Play More House. Please dubstep please (wink). Take me backstage. All human life is here. And some inhuman. Enjoy.

Bill Brewster

djhistory.com
Co-Author, "Last Night A DJ Saved My Life",
"How To DJ (Properly)"
and "The Record Players: DJ Revolutionaries"

A few years ago, I was spinning at a club in Chinatown, Los Angeles...

...where my DJ partner Henry Self and I are residents. Right around last call, we noticed someone who looked exactly like Britney Spears on the dancefloor.

It's a disco night with a pretty flamboyant crowd, so it's not unheard-of to see guys dressed in drag like Britney Spears walk around the club snapping their fingers, saying "It's Britney, bitch!" We looked a little closer and it was, in fact, Britney Spears. And holy shit, Lindsay Lohan too! Just hanging out...and dancing...at our club. It was great. They even got the venue to stay open past the usual Los Angeles 2AM closing time.

Eventually, Britney walks up to the turntables and asks me and Henry to "play some Madonna or old-school MJ". Because of the type of night it was, playing some classic Michael Jackson fit in perfectly. So we busted out an MJ track (I can't remember which one), and Britney, LiLo and everyone else continued to dance their asses off.

We didn't play her request because she had breasts, contrary to the title of this book. We played it because it was a good idea and fit in with the vibe of the night. Now, I'm not a fan of hers or her music, but I am a big fan of her approach to requesting a song.

I actually appreciate requests, if they work within my set. And I usually play them, if I have it. Part of our job as DJs is to play what people want, and requests are a direct line to my peeps on the dancefloor. Of course, another part of our job is to lead the way and play music they've never heard before — songs that they will love so much, they'll come back and request the next night.

But, let's face it, a lot of times requests are terrible. Or the people demanding the requests are not exactly nice about it. How is a DJ supposed to react to a sweaty punter charging the DJ booth and demanding, "When are you gonna play something good?" or "Can you play something I can dance to?" Ironically, these questions are usually asked while the dancefloor is PACKED. So, uh, no I'm not gonna play grindcore at a disco night. Or Mariah Carrey at a goth night. Or Gangnam Style...any night!

Because it tends to get loud in clubs, many of these outrageous requests are written down on anything people can find — cocktail napkins, coasters, beer bottle labels, dollar bills — and handed to the DJ. Sometimes, they get ignored and thrown in the trash.

Well, nowadays, they get photographed and blasted all over the internet.

"No Breasts No Requests" is a unique collection of these requests, as well as other notes and signs found in DJ booths all over the world. First gathered on *NoBreastsNoRequests.tumblr.com* back in 2010...and now in this book that you are holding in your hands.

All of the photos have been found online or submitted by friends, fans or fellow DJs. None of this would be possible without their contribution, and for that, I am eternally grateful and dedicate this book to them. And also to everyone else who loves the nightlife and appreciates great music — whether they are playing it, listening to it, or dancing their asses off to it like Britney Spears.

Mick DiMaria

DJ Mick Fiction

When Clubgoers Attack!

For the most part, if people don't like what the DJ is playing, they just don't dance. Or they hit the bar, go for a smoke on the patio, or worst case, leave the club.

But there are a select few who take it a step further. They march right up to the booth and let the DJ know exactly how they feel by stealthily scribbling it down on a piece of paper and passing it to the DJ. Probably while he or she is in mid-mix and unable to read it while the person is standing right there. Yes, it can be passive-aggressive. Often times, a little more emphasis on 'aggressive.'

Some of these notes are direct insults. Some suggest a change in career. And some are just straight-up death threats! These are the people who take The Smiths' "Hang the DJ" a little too literally.

Why? Maybe because people spend a lot of their hard-earned money to get into a club. And, right or wrong, they expect a lot in terms of entertainment and hearing what they want to hear. But, even though it is the club or bar promoter who hires the DJ, many patrons feel they are the boss and the DJs are their own personal iPods.

The flowing alcohol at the bar and the half-price drink specials definitely don't help. Booze makes people brave and say things they normally would not. Drinks may help get the body moving and get people on the dancefloor, but Happy Hour is not always so happy for the DJ.

Clubgoers sometimes try to soften the blow of a really hardcore insult with cute, little drawings. But little hearts or smiley faces just don't buy back the damage of the words "YOU SUCK AND I WISH YOU WOULD DIE" in all caps.

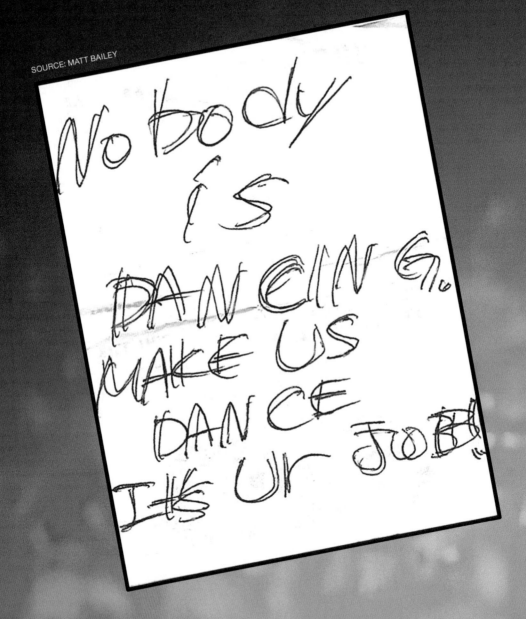

Hey, do I go to Burger King and
tell YOU how to do YOUR job?

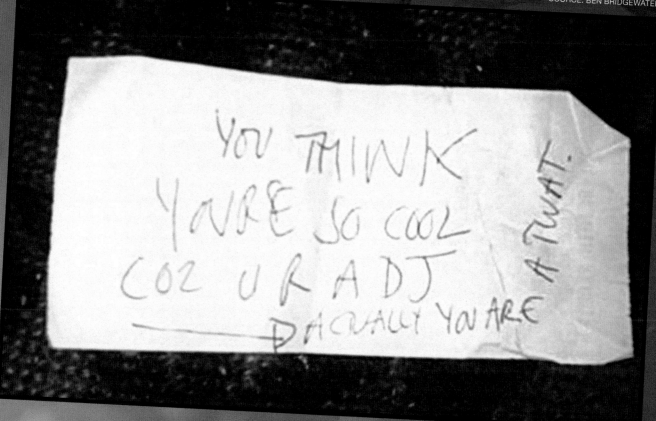

Somebody had an extra helping of hater tots.

Subtle.

YOU ARE HORRIBLE everybody

But how do you really feel?

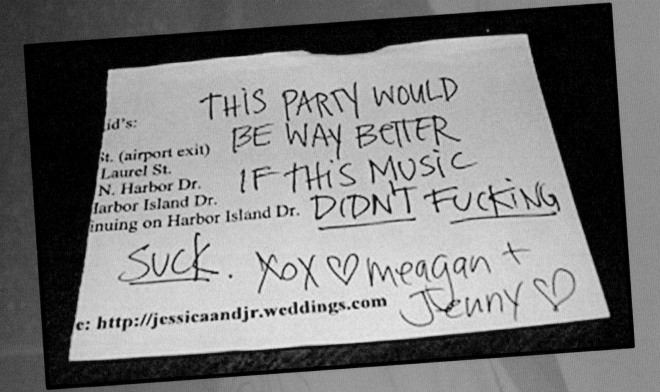

DJ-ing: You're doing it wrong.

You as the DJ Sucks ass when it Comes to playin Good music

And you as a douchebag sucks ass when it comes to writtin GOOD English.

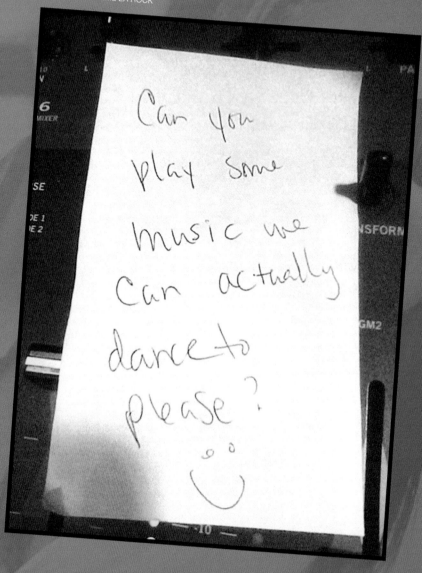

Pretty much the most insulting thing you could say to a DJ.
And no, the smiley face does not make it okay.

Can You Play Some better Shit soon? Kaskade? Don Rimini Hearts Revolution? Cyndi laupers new cd's. Recent? xo gossipgirl.

Cyndi Lauper is recent?

Translation: I HATE DANCE MUSIC.

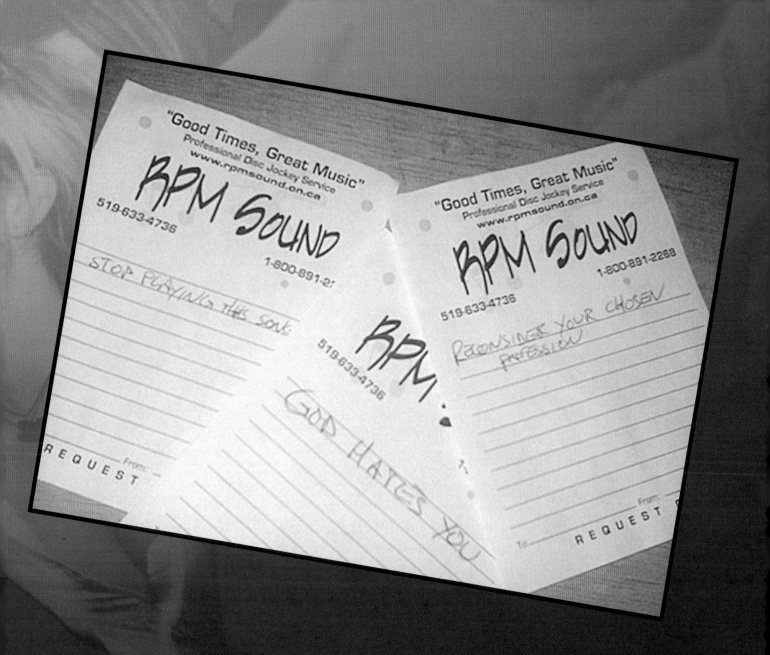

"That's funny...I've never heard of any of these songs"
—A clueless DJ

TODAY WAS THE <u>WORST</u> DISPLAY OF DJ-ing IN THE HISTORY OF MUSIC!!!

Found at a Paris Hilton gig?

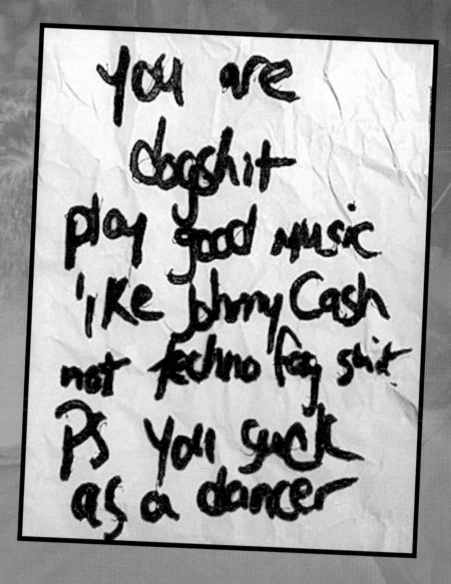

Because nothing gets people dancing in a
techno club like Johnny Cash.

Dear DJ,

"Like a G6" is a hip + cool song.

I think you should reconsider the "vibe" you're looking for...

Hip people love NEW music vs. Michael Jackson, Commodores and Will Smith

Love,
THE TABLE of cool people! ♡

Tables full of "hip, cool people" can go straight to hell.

SOURCE: DJP

Crushing insults aren't so bad
on a heart shaped Post-it® note.

TO: DJ

FROM: ≤ω

MESSAGE:
Condescending Prick. w/ horrible taste in music.
Wake up dude! your a bar DJ get off your high horse
AND your dick is small

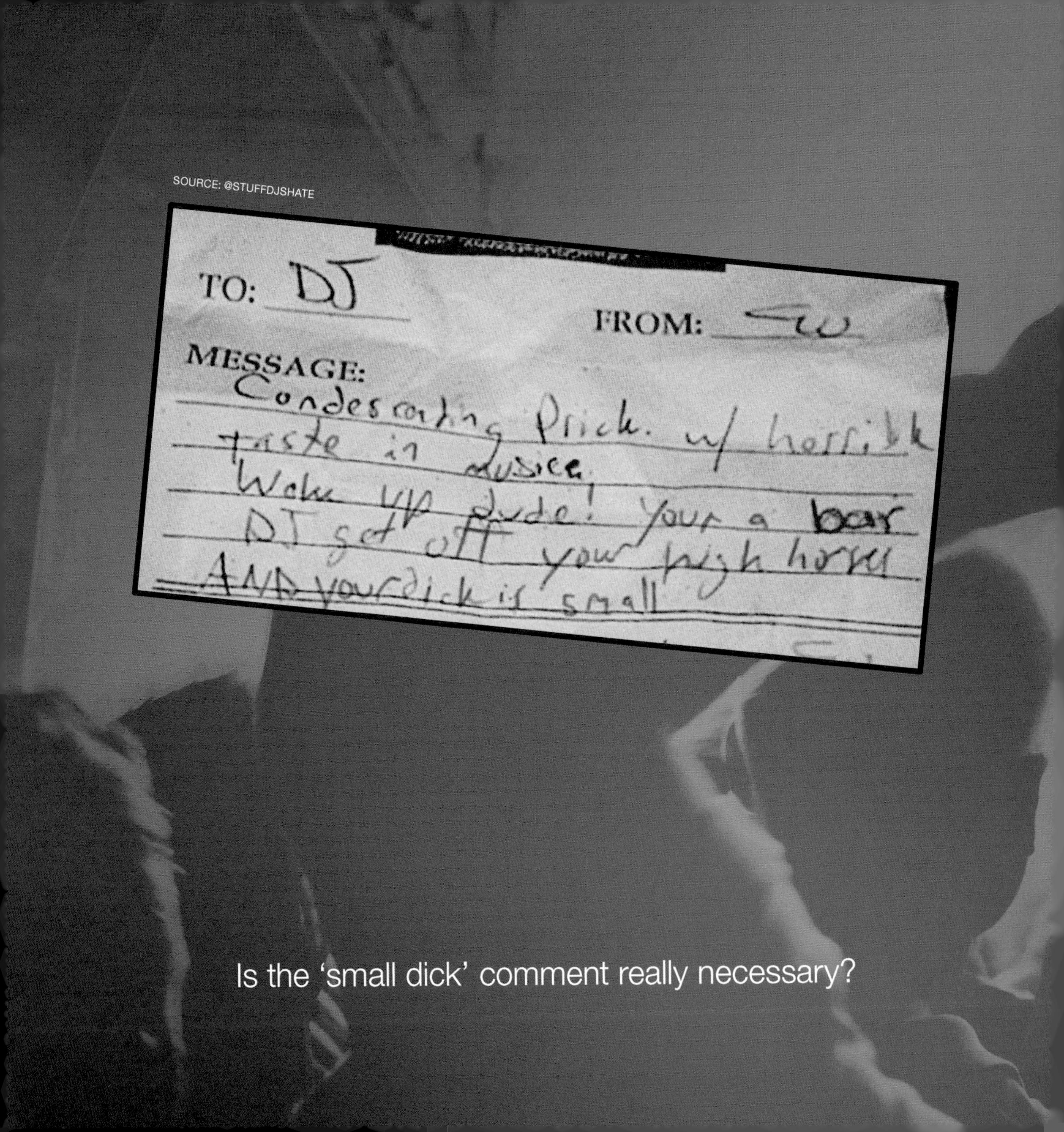

Is the 'small dick' comment really necessary?

4... 4... 4 insults in 1!

Money Talks

For every superstar DJ making millions of dollars and headlining Las Vegas, there are thousands upon thousands of DJs just making ends meet. So when a request comes in with a little cashola attached, that gets some attention.

Now that doesn't mean that if the song sucks or does not fit within the set, they should play it (some still do). But it does mean it will get considered a little bit more or get played a little bit quicker.

Sure, some DJs may feel a bit like a human jukebox when someone pays them to play a song. After all, the club is already paying them and, if your request is solid, it shouldn't need to come with money. But DJs tend to get over that pretty quick.

Sometimes the request is written right on the money itself. Technically, that's defacing money and is punishable by, um, probably nothing. But it does make for some noteworthy notes. And probably some confused cashiers at the local grocery store afterwards ("Sooo… you want to *buy* some Black Eyed Peas?")

"Sorry, a dollar will only get you Vanilla Ice and a chuckle."

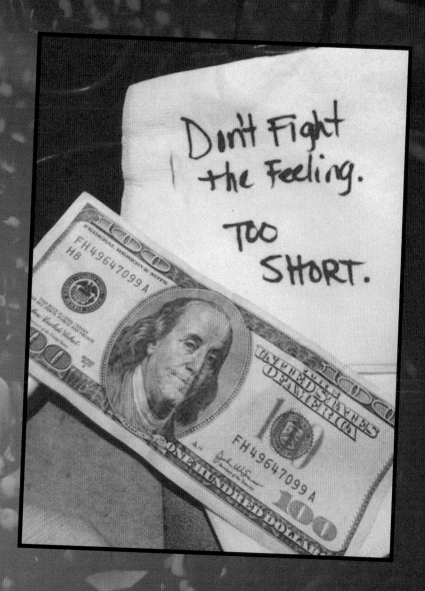

100 very compelling reasons to play Too $hort.

20 baht = 75 cents = FAIL

- REQUESTS - $20.⁰⁰
- "PLAY IT NEXT" - $50.⁰⁰
- "PLAY IT NEXT" (BUT IT SUCKS) - $100.⁰⁰
- JUSTIN BIEBER - $1000.⁰⁰
- DUBSTEP - MAKE ME AN OFFER! ☺

The official DJ request price chart.

This is either a request for the Enrique Iglesias song...
or George Washington is a hornier President than Bill Clinton.

Chocolate coins aren't just for overweight strippers.
This one given to a DJ in Stockholm ("muta" is Swedish for bribe).

Sex For Songs

There are some people who like to give money in exchange for getting their song played. And some people…like to give sex. Oral sex. Regular sex. Threesome, foursome or fivesome sex. Even just the potential for poontang is enough to do the trick.

In any case, it's usually very well received by the mostly-male DJ community. And it's usually a sure-fire way to get your song played ASAP.

Does that mean the dirty deed ends up happening? Probably not. But if you hear the DJ skip a beat behind the decks, something might be going on underneath the turntables.

A few horn-dog DJs have taken to even posting signs by the booth requesting "compensation" for requests. BJs seem to be a popular form of payment.

But what about the ladies? There are plenty of female DJs out there. Forget "No Breasts, No Requests" – how about "No Dicks, No Mix"? Kinda has a ring to it. Though not sure we'll be seeing signs around the DJ booth anytime soon that say 'Show Us Your Balls!"

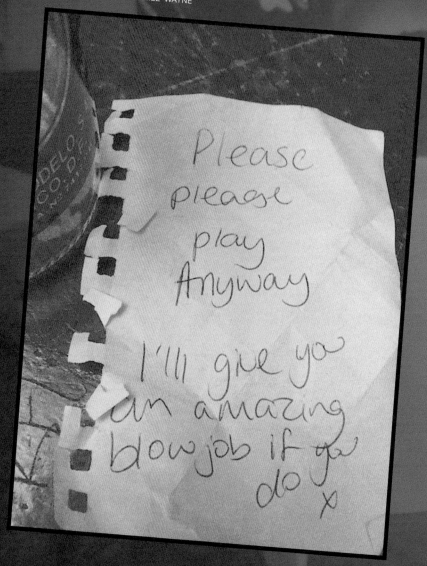

How To Get A DJ's Attention: Lesson One

do you wanna have a 4-some tonight? If you play "we built this city," that will happen.

If you build it, they will come.

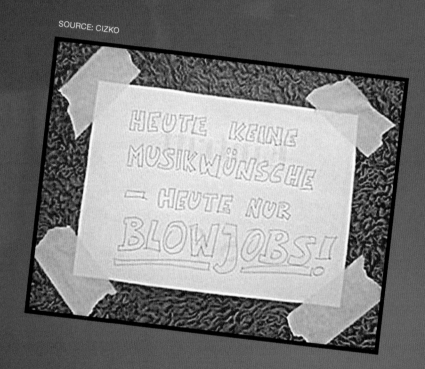

In German: "TODAY NO REQUESTS, JUST BLOWJOBS!"
Assuming they mean 'receiving'.

This person really wanted to hear Mariah Carey.

Technically, still a request.

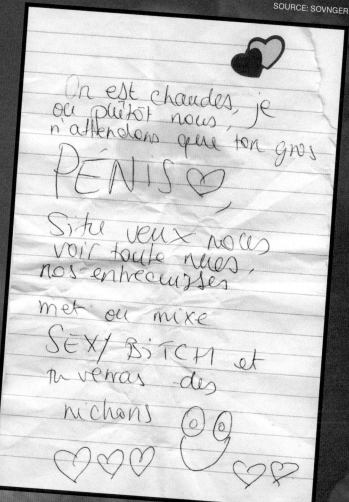

In French: "We are hot, I or rather we are waiting for your big PENIS, if you want to see us naked, our crotch, play or mix Sexy Bitch and you will see tits!"

Sounds legit.

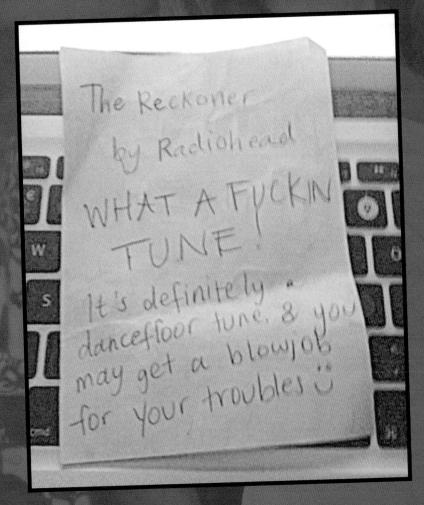

Radio-head.

Anyyyyyy-thing?

MUSIKWÜNSCHE
NUR NACH MÜNDLICHER ABSPRACHE

In German: "REQUESTS ONLY
AFTER ORAL CONSULTATION"

Drugs 'n Alcohol

Drugs and alcohol go hand-in-hand with music and nightclubs. You could say that one enhances the other. From the parties of today to the raves, discos and Woodstocks of yesterday.

Yeah, there are people who don't imbibe, partake or indulge. They're called designated drivers. Or people in AA.

But for the most part, drugs and alcohol are part of club life and influence much of what happens in the environment – inside and outside the DJ booth.

Inside the booth, it's all about the drink tickets. These little tokens of joy from the promoter or bar owner are almost as important as actually getting paid with money. A liquid currency, if you will. But don't spill any of that liquid currency on the club equipment or you may get fucked up in a whole different way.

Outside the booth, well, let's just say that friends shouldn't let friends drink 'n request. Like car keys, if you see your friend drunkenly scribbling a nonsensical request on a piece of scrap paper, just take away the pen.

Most of the time, the note is completely unreadable. Who knows if it's even a song request! Maybe it's because, in our society, we're so used to texting and typing that we forget how to properly write by hand. Or maybe it's because, in a club, it's so dark and smoky that we can barely see two feet in front of us.

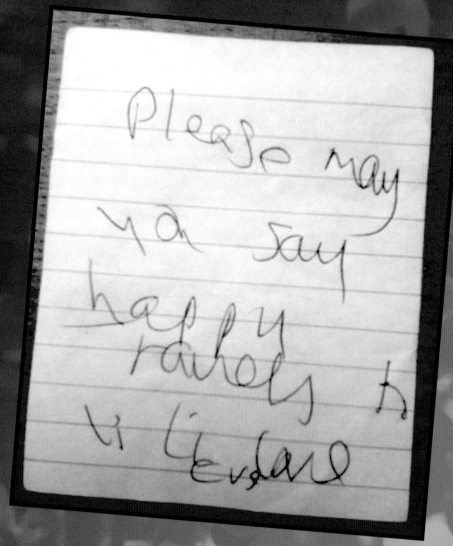

Go home, pen. You're drunk.

DJ I TAKE SOME DRUGS.. CAN U HELP ME WITH YOUR MUSIC!

Yes.

Could you mind to play "House music" like DJ (cause my friends already drunk) She need to Dance.

Thank you.

Your "friend" is drunk? Riiiiiiight.

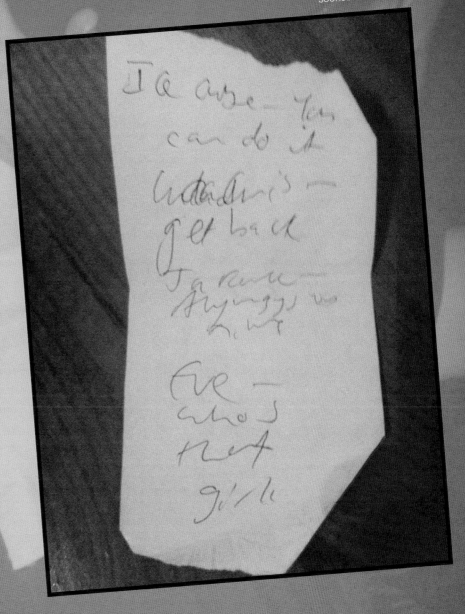

Requesting Under the Influence.

Thankfully, the Management
was only referring to drinking wine.

SPILL A DRINK, I SPILL YOUR BLOOD! ♡ FANTANA

PBR = R.I.P.

"Do You Have Any Hip Hop?"

t doesn't matter if it's a house party, a club, a Bat Mitzvah or an underground eather bar, someone will inevitably ask the DJ to play hip hop. Sometimes it's a specific song. Or sometimes it's the entire genre. Which is fine. Hip hop is probably he most popular style of music in the world, so it's not a huge surprise.

But as many DJs have realized: Once you go hip hop, you can never go back. That's not to say you can't jump around from genre to genre and go from hip hop to other music. You can. Though not too many people wanna hear Siouxsie & The Banshees after Erik B. & Rakim. You've given them the beat, the bass and the hooks — and hat shit's usually a one-way street.

t's not a black or white thing. It's just a thing. Almost everyone loves hip hop, from he kids in the city to the kids in the 'burbs. And not in the way that most of the population likes country music. Country…not so big in the inner city clubs.

So get ready DJs, whether your laptop is loaded with hip hop or not, be prepared to field requests from all shades of people for all kinds of reasons – birthdays, engagements, or just because that really drunk white dude wants to "freestyle" over a "dope beat" on the "mic."

It socks when you get notes like this.
Makes you feel really krappy.

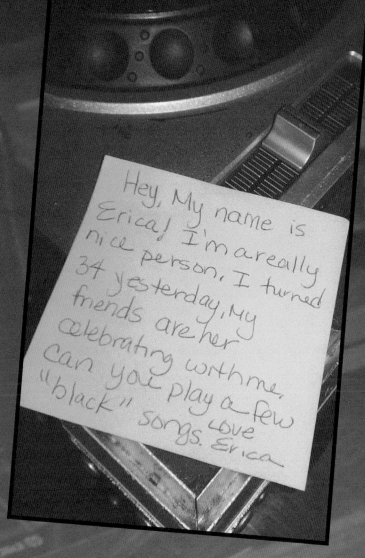

"How 'bout a DAS RACIST track?"

Because nothing says romance like a Pitbull song.

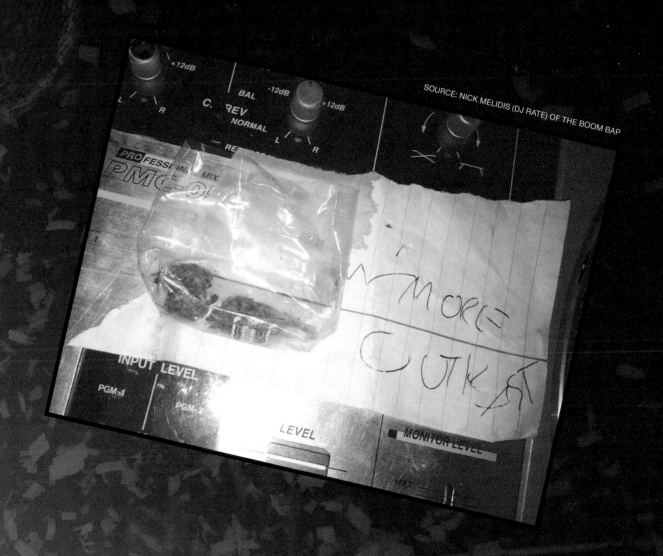

This is how to get the DJ to play Outkast immediately.

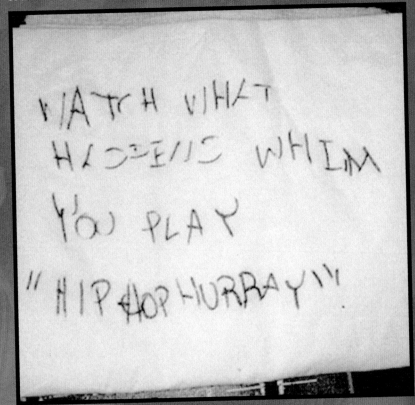

Uh…what happens? You get magically
transported back to Spring Break 1993?

Please avoid saying something stupid

such as:

"when are you going to play hip hop?"

It's ok to think outside of the box

& by the way, it's called HOUSE MUSIC, not Techno!

Thank you!

Black guys like rap. Who knew?

OK, one more you dear boy.
Tiffany is having a
b-day too. Maybe

AKon – Smack That
or ~~Fergielove~~ Fergielicious!

♡ you!

Strike 1: Calling the DJ "dear boy".
Strike 2: Another birthday request from the same person in one night.
Strike 3: Akon.

The Odd, Morbid & Bizarre

Every once in a while, someone rolls up to the DJ booth with a request so strange and so personal, it stops the DJ in his or her tracks. Like, literally makes the record skip. Not because of the song, necessarily, but because of the situation. It can be the ultimate in T.M.I.

If you ever need proof that truth is stranger than fiction, hang out by the turntables for a few hours and witness some of these head-scratchers.

Some of them make you think that the clubgoer is more in need of a therapist than a DJ. Or the Mayo Clinic instead of Ministry of Sound. Pain-numbing drugs instead of pain-numbing dru— ohhh wait a minute, maybe there are more similarities than differences.

The point is, whether it's all a fantasy or not, the bar/club/dancefloor is supposed to be a happy place. It's all part of the fake utopia we buy into when we pay the cover charge and walk into a place where regular reality bullshit doesn't matter as much. But sometimes, the sadness can't help but peek its somber little head inside.

Well, thanks to bar napkins and the backs of pharmacy receipts, these bizarre, gloomy and sometimes scary messages have been captured for your twisted and perverse enjoyment. I hope you're happy with yourselves.

Great. Another shit request. Hope the person who wrote this saved the napkin. You know, just in case.

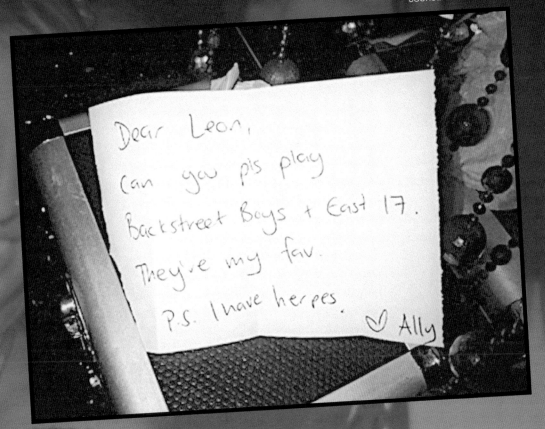

Dear Leon,
Can you pls play
Backstreet Boys + East 17.
They're my fav.
P.S. I have herpes.
♡ Ally

Worst request and worst P.S. of all-time.

10 - Second brake between
Songs So ~~yes~~ a person
can politely take leave
of a partner They
don't wish to continue
Dancing with —

Might as well just plug in the iPod at this point.

Rubstep?

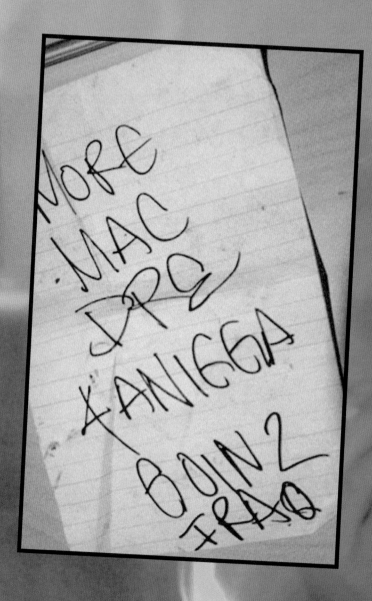

Don't Request, Don't Tell.

Hey Dude,

You really rock, where do you take these songs from? Steve Aoki? hahaha! I would really love to ~~download~~ buy music from you! Do you have any web or facebook? See you!

Felipe Bravo.

Priceless on so many levels.

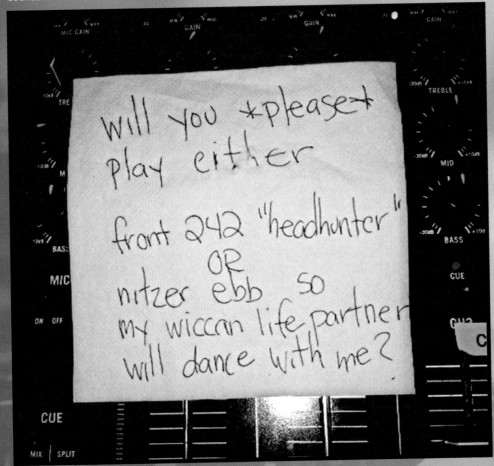

Goths are so romantic.

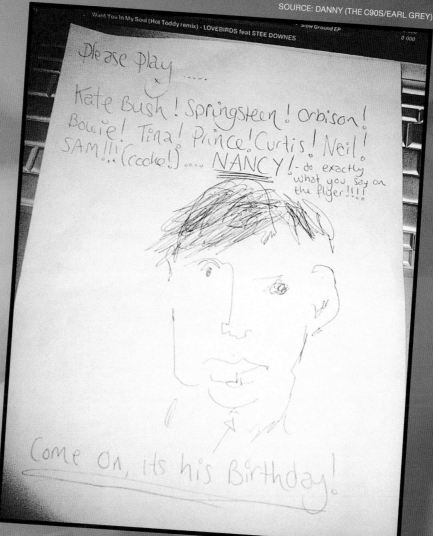

The most frightening birthday request ever received.

The No-Play List

Okay, enough talk about what people want DJs to play. Let's talk about what people, including the DJs themselves, do NOT want to play. Everrrrr.

It's usually the massively overplayed songs by the massively overpaid artists. They change from year to year, and some are specific to a certain club, but many of them are universal. You know which ones they are. A few of them even have dances associated with them. But pretty much all of these songs have choruses that get stuck in our collective heads, whether we like it or not, which is probably the reason we both love AND hate them.

Surely, some DJs take pride in never playing *that* song…and like to brag about it. And some clubs make it a point to list the songs, artists, and even genres that they don't want spun in their clubs. This is not one of those things coming from the crowd, it's more internal.

So here are the songs and artists DJs spin at their own risk. They are the anti-request. Play them and there might be blood.

That number can never be too high. #PlayMeNever

SOURCE: JUAN MACLEAN

DJ's:
NO HIP HOP
NO DUBSTEP
NO LMFAO

No LMFAO = LMFAO!

BACKGROUND SOURCE: SMPLSTC (FLICKR)

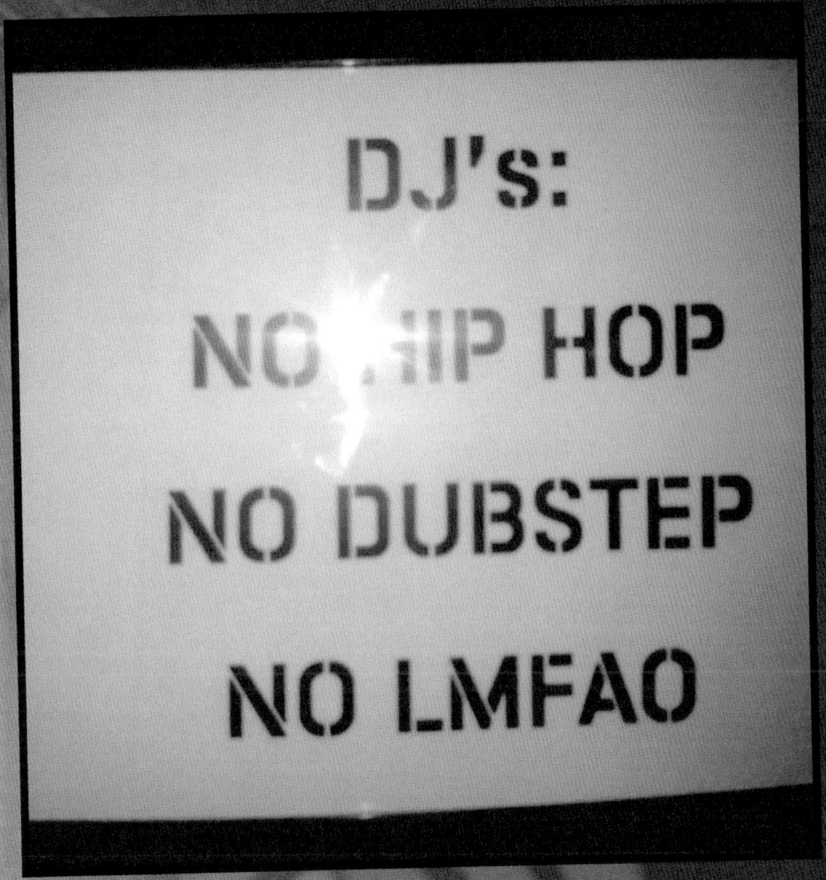

Message to all DJ's

There is not to be any version of <u>cinema</u> played tonight!

& fuck it levels is banned too.
(includes all remix's skrillex backward etc)

Anyone that plays these songs will be kicked in the vaginal area and thrown off the roof.

Don't drop the bass.

NO LADY GAGA!!!
You Play, You Pay! It
will be turned off; your
$ will not be returned!

THIS IS YOUR WARNING

Sorry, little monsters.

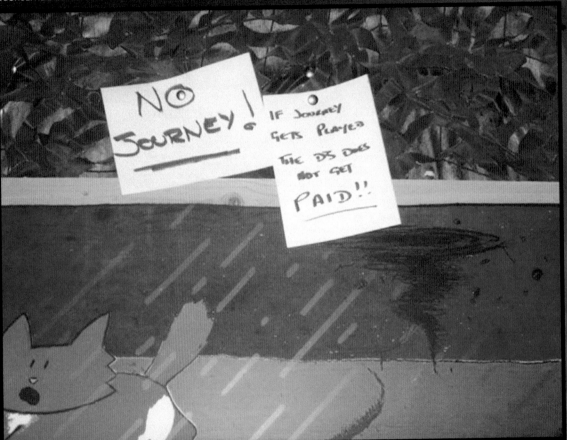

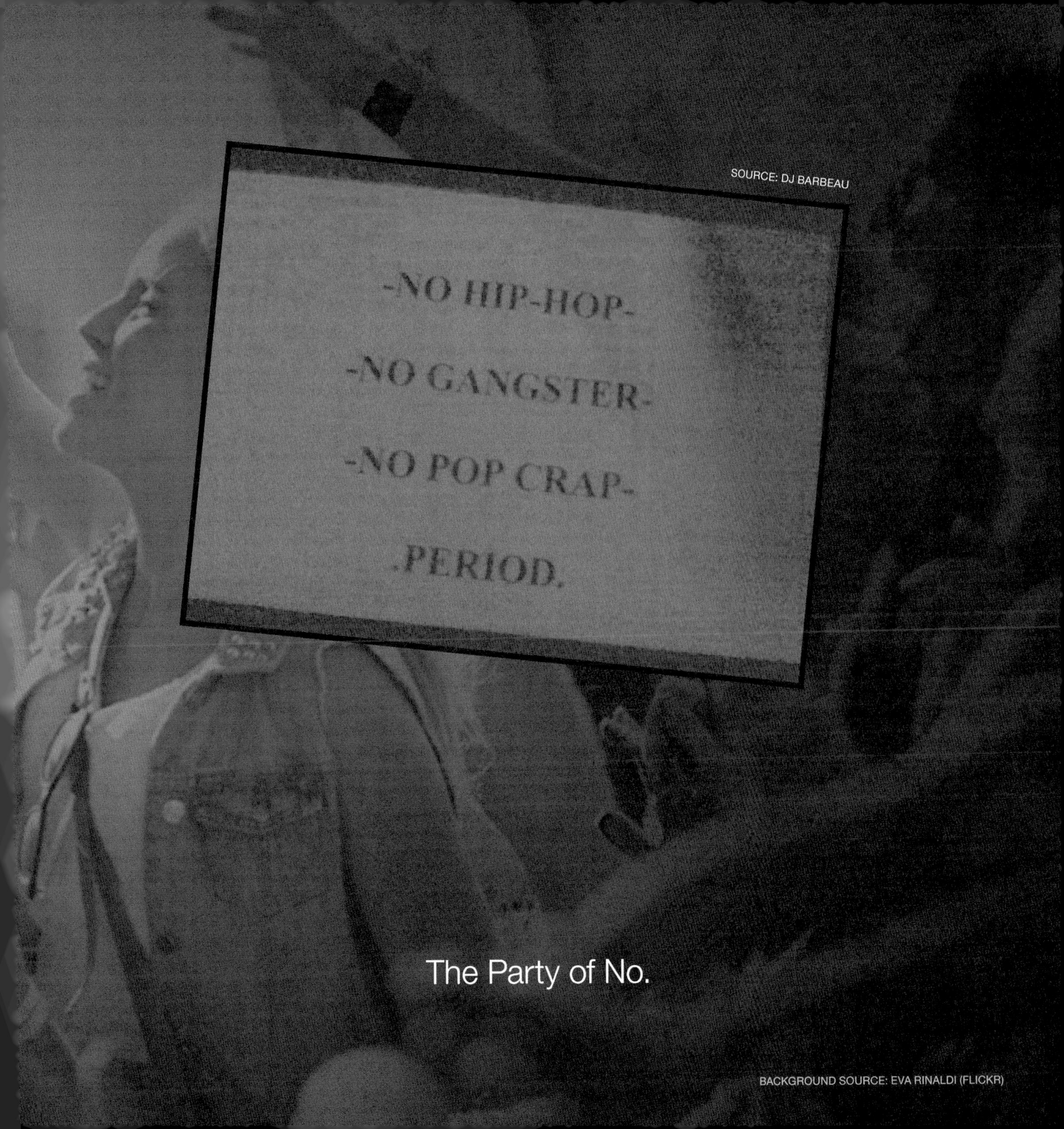

-NO HIP-HOP-
-NO GANGSTER-
-NO POP CRAP-
-PERIOD.

SOURCE: DJ BARBEAU

The Party of No.

BACKGROUND SOURCE: EVA RINALDI (FLICKR)

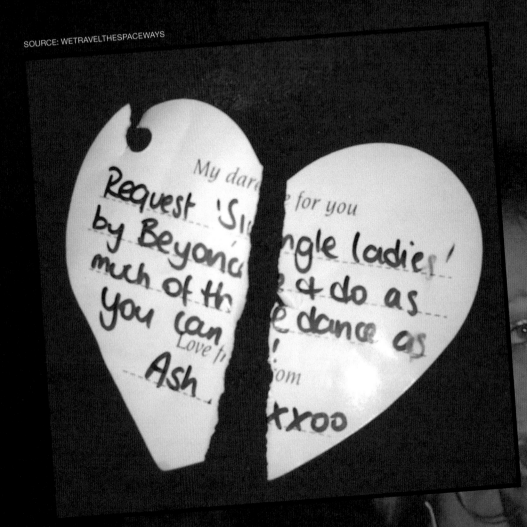

The only proper response after receiving a request like this.

"Came in really handy in the Summer of 2010!!"

Could've probably guessed this by the environment.

WER HEUTE ABEND
ETWAS VON
DAVID GUETTA SPIELT,
BEKOMMT ÜBEL AUFS MAUL
UND WIRD HINTERM
HAUS VERGRABEN!

TRANSLATION: "Whoever plays David Guetta tonight gets badly smacked in the face and buried behind the house!"

Never mess with the Germans!

From The Management...

Clearly, notes in the DJ booth aren't just limited to requests from clubgoers. Many notes left for the DJ are from the club owners themselves. They could be directed at the DJ or to everyone in the entire club.

These guys are busy. Owners or promoters are at the venue almost every night. And, generally speaking, they're not there to party. Therefore, they get right to business and may not have time to be polite all the time. So when they don't like something or have rules they want to enforce, up goes a note on the wall.

And it's not just from the management, it's also from the sound guys. Sound guys can be a DJ's best friend — they can help control the sound and levels in the club to make sure everyone enjoys the music. But they, too, can be a little gruff. Violent threats and/or involuntary castration for messing with "their" equipment are not uncommon.

You'd think a place as open and free as a nightclub wouldn't have so many rules… but they do. No coats in the booth. No moshing on the dancefloor. No audio levels in the red. No sex in the Champagne Room.

This is a DJ booth

Not a place to hang out

If you want to party

There's a nightclub quite close

The DJ booth at a club is like the kitchen at a house party…everyone always seems to end up there.

NO MOBILES ON THE DANCEFLOOR, PLEASE

IT KILLS THE VIBE AND MAKES YOU LOOK LIKE A BORING BASTARD

You know who you are.

And if you don't know, now you know.

IF YOU ARE
DANCING IN A WAY
THAT COULD
CREATE A
BABY/FETUS/ALIEN

.....

STOP.

IT IS NOT BEHOOVING OF YOU AND
AWKWARD.

Is there any other way to dance?

No BreakDancing
on the
lighted
Dance Floor

BreakDancing
Upstairs

Well, obviously.

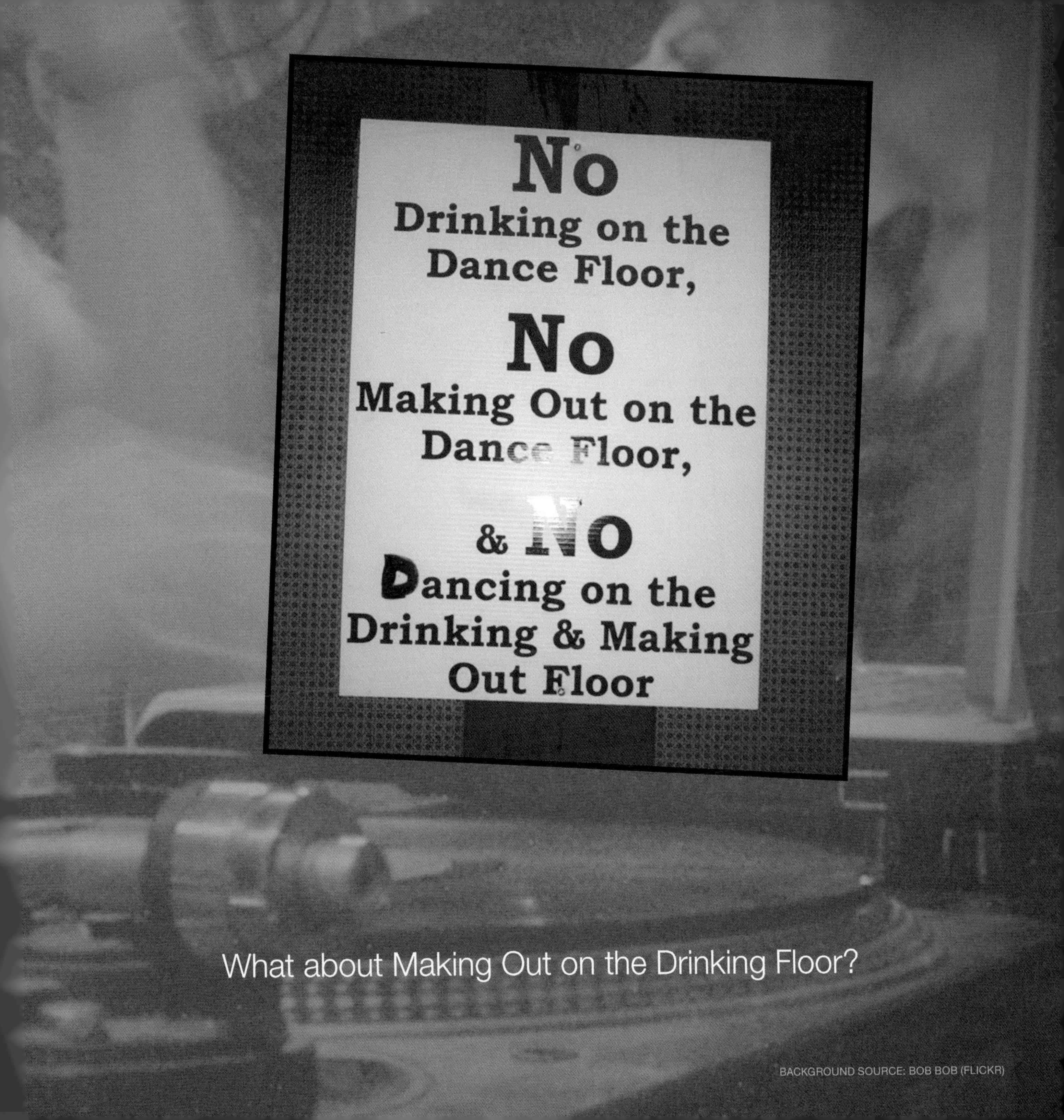

No
Drinking on the
Dance Floor,

No
Making Out on the
Dance Floor,

& NO
Dancing on the
Drinking & Making
Out Floor

What about Making Out on the Drinking Floor?

ATTN ALL DJ's & FRIENDS: DON'T GET ON THE MIC IF YOU SOUND LIKE A DUMBASS. ANY SWEARING OR DUMB COMMENTS WILL GET YOU KICKED OUT OF THE CLUB. I DON'T CARE WHO YOU ARE. BE SMART, DON'T TRY AND "RAP" OR SAY "UHH-OHH" YOU JUST LOOK STUPID. THANKS ☺ -RYAN

Truth.

DJ 50 SONG SET
WHEN IN DOUBT PLAY OFF THIS LIST!!

AC/DC	You Shook Me All Night Long
Aha	Call on me
Belinda Carlisle	Heaven is a place on earth
Billy Idol	Dancing with myself
Billy Ocean	Billy ocean get out of my dream
Black Eyed Peas	Let's Get It Started
Black Eyed Peas	Pump It
Black Eyed Peas	I gotta feeling
Black Eyed Peas	Boom boom pow
Bob Marley	
Bon Jovi	Livin' On A Prayer
Def Leppard	Pour Some Sugar On Me
Diamond, Neil	Sweet Caroline (Good Times Never Seemed So Good)
Eddie Money	Take me home tonight
George Michael	Faith
Grandmaster Flash	The message
Guns N' Roses	Sweet Child O' Mine
Hey Champ	Cold hearted girl
Idol, Billy	Mony Mony
Jackson, Michael	Billie Jean
Jackson, Michael	Thriller
Jackson, Michael	Don't Stop Til You Get Enough
Jay z	Run this town
Journey	Don't Stop Believin'
Katy Perry	Katy Perry
Keri Hilson	Knock you down
Lady Gaga	The fame
Lady Gaga	Love Game
Lady Gaga	Poker Face
Lauper, Cyndi	Girls Just Want To Have Fun
Madonna	Like A Prayer
Madonna	Holiday
Marvin Gaye	Sexual Healing
Pat Benatar	
Prince	Kiss
Pussycat Dolls	I hate this part or Bottle pop
Rihanna	Don't Stop The Music
Rihanna Feat. Jay-Z	Umbrella
T.I.	Whatever you like
The Ramones	I wanna be sedated
The Ting Tings	That's not my name
The Ting Tings	Shut up and let me go
Tiffany	I think we're alone now
Timberlake, Justin	Sexyback
Van Halen	
Whitney Houston	How would I know

Song #51: "Kill Me Now" by Every DJ In The World

PLAYING IN DOUBLE RED WILL INSTANTLY TRANSFORM YOU INTO JUSTIN BIEBER

If this doesn't scare you into
keeping it in the yellow, nothing will.

DO NOT LEAVE
ANY BAGS
COATS OR
GIRLFRIENDS IN
THE DJ BOOTH

USE THE
CLOAKROOM
BOTTOM OF
STAIRS

The cloakroom sounds like more fun.

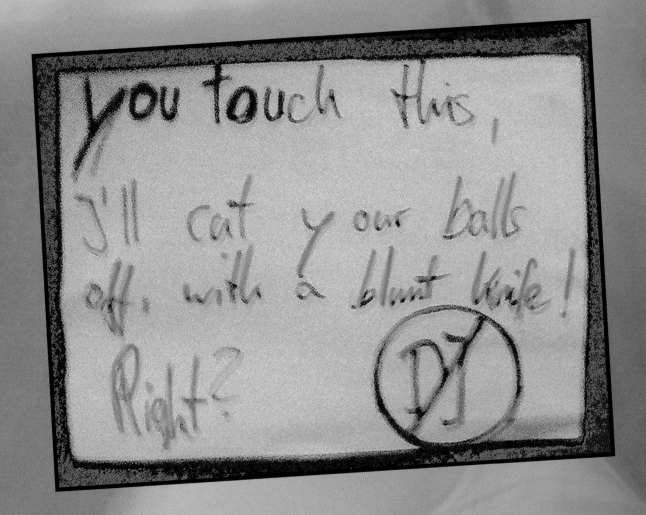

Lighting guys are just the best.

The crowd is party group. Dance Music Please NOT HOUSE!

High End Casino Please Remember

House Music All Night Wrong?

you are our bitch
-C

Whoever the Cunt is that put the mic in the downstairs claset and its respective XLR cable in the upstairs closet -- Fuck you. I hope you die in a fire.

There's a special place in hell reserved for people who separate audio components.

Turn up the bass, get punched in the face.

Attention
The next person
that touches the
lighting desk, I will
personally choke
them out, then
throw them down
the fucking stairs,
hoping that they
break their neck.

Malcolm.

Malcolm needs a hug.

The More You Know.™...

Compliments

These are, by far, the rarest of notes passed along to the DJ. Yes, they happen. And yes, DJs receive other forms of positive affirmation that they're doing well (like the dancing hordes of people having a good time on the dancefloor...or the nod – the unspoken tip o' the hat to the man or woman on the 1s and 2s telling them, "hey, good job mate.")

These notes are like the 'thank you' cards of clubland and the handwritten version of a high-five on a cocktail napkin. If and when DJs get them, they should keep them and cherish them always. As did the DJs on the following pages. Nice mix! Nice tune! Nice ass! Whatever the message, they're appreciated.

These words of encouragement help offset the rude notes. Because after all, we are all human, and it's always better to be called "THE shit" instead of just "shit."

Do mothers or fathers or other family members related to the DJs anonymously slip these into the DJ booth? Maybe. But a compliment is a compliment. And DJs, with all the criticism they get, deserve to be told "hey, good job mate" every once in a while.

This Note About This Song Fuckin' Rocks!

So much more pleasant than the usual "U R A CUNT."

UR DeeJaying 16-07-11
is Entertainingly
Enjoyable & Most
importantly
Dance Able thanx
-THERESA - Danced All Nite xx

Notes like these are enjoyable and
most importantly awesomeable.

u R to good to play in this SHITHOLE !!.

Have you got YMCA !

The song request kinda cancels out the compliment.

I haven't herd this song since ages

You made my night

Lets have a drink after your set. ♡

Too good to be true?

Don't usually see "cute" and "AC/DC" in the same sentence.

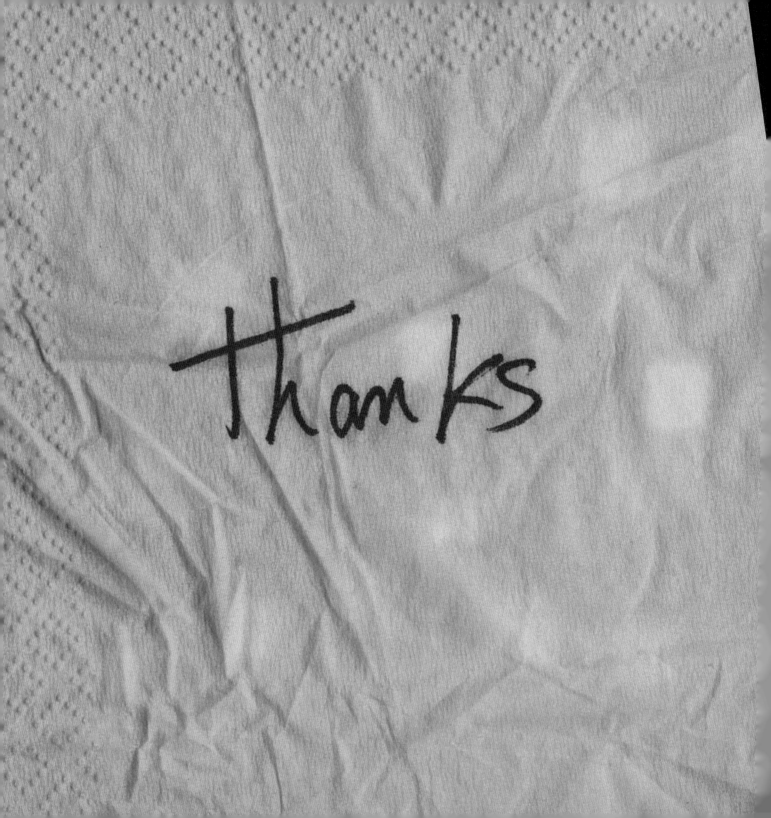

Shout-Outs

Mick DiMaria would like to thank his wife Mary Ann for the love, support and for putting up with the name of this project all this time - and kids Dylan and Jake, who aren't allowed to read this book for a few more years. Henry Self, my DJ partner-in-crime, for the legal help and proofreading. Walter May for inspiring me to turn the blog into a book. John "Coco" Lopez for convincing me to actually do it myself and for his beautiful design and production skillz. My amazing agent Amy Tipton for always believing in me and this book when not many others did and for all her tireless efforts in making it a reality. Brad Getty from "Dads Are The Original Hipsters" for the helpful advice and Tom Pariso from "StuffDJsHate" for the support. Dimitri From Paris, Paul Oakenfold and Kissy Sell Out for the kind words. Mixmag, Vice, Dazed, Rolling Stone, Beatport, Gizmodo, Don't Panic, BuzzFeed and inthemix for the props. Captains of Industry and Supreme La Rock who began collecting notes like these well before I did. The legendary Bill Brewster for writing the Foreword for this book. Tumblr for creating such an awesome and easy platform that almost any idiot (i.e. me) can use and the sick, twisted, cool, creative and still somewhat underground Tumblr community for accepting me as one of their own. And most importantly, a big Thank You to all the people who have submitted their photos of notes, signs and requests throughout the years and made this thing what it is today.

John Lopez would like to thank his loving wife Jill and son Maxwell for the encouragement, support, and for tolerating the late nights. Additional thanks to Maxwell and Michael for keeping me young on the inside while my beard is going gray. Many thanks to the wonderfully creative photographers who have the courage to trust others with their work via Creative Commons licenses. And of course, my thanks to Mick for the half-dozen glasses of whisky that got us talking about this in the first place.